D1357319

The English Electric Lightning Story

The English Electric Lightning Story

Martin W. Bowman

The
History
Press

Also in this series:

The Concorde Story

The Spitfire Story

The Vulcan Story

The Red Arrows Story

The Harrier Story

The Dam Busters Story

The Hurricane Story

The Lifeboat Story

The Tornado Story

The Hercules Story

Published in the United Kingdom in 2010 by
The History Press
The Mill · Brimscombe Port · Stroud · Gloucestershire · GL5 2QG

British Library Cataloguing in Publication Data
A catalogue record for this book is available from the British Library.

Hardback ISBN 978-0-7524-5080-3

Typesetting and origination by The History Press
Printed in Italy by L.E.G.O. S.p.A.

Half title page: *See page 28.*

Title page: *See page 31.*

CONTENTS

Introduction   06

Background   08

Into Service   19

Tigers, T-Birds and the Firebirds   36

QRA   48

Tiger Trails and Tanking with the Tanker Trash   56

The Power   75

And the Glory   88

The Magic Carpet Ride   107

Appendix 1 Specifications   113

Appendix 2 Milestones   116

Small boys, it is said, want to be engine drivers. Trains never really made the same lasting impression on me that the 'jet age' did. The early 1960s were the days before political correctness, when the sounds of the sixties were easy on the airwaves and the only foreign footballers came from Wales, Ireland and Scotland. A new 1968 Vauxhall Viva 90 (de luxe!) cost just £744 and your Morris Oxford Traveller came in Trafalgar Blue. Car tyres were only £3 17s 6d in real money. In Norwich in 1968 a 'modern detached bungalow', just three years old, was 'only' £3,350, while a spacious detached house cost just £750 more. All right, so you were on £14 a week and probably had to work for two or three months to buy a decent camera. However, if, during school holidays, you stood at the yellow crash gate at RAF Coltishall to witness the English Electric Lightning, the last all-British fighter aircraft, take off with full reheat, then you too would recall these days with affection. Perhaps the most spectacular item in the Lightning repertoire was the rotation take off: the seemingly vertical climb with the aircraft supported on two invisible but ear shattering columns of thrust was an unforgettable sight. As Group Captain David Seward, OC, 56 Firebirds Squadron, once said: 'The aeroplane was superb to fly, a bitch to maintain and always short of fuel. In hindsight, we probably wouldn't have wanted it any other way.' Another favourite recollection of mine, which has become the stuff of legend, goes: 'I had control of the aircraft all the way until I released the brakes.'

No one can ever take away the vivid memories of the cacophony of sound generated by the twin Avons, which reverberated around the airfield like a violent storm. Afternoons at the 'pictures' and balmy days watching the electrifying Lightnings have long since gone by. Although four Lightnings are owned and operated by Thunder City in South Africa, Bruntingthorpe Airfield in Leicestershire is now the only place in Britain where one can see a Lightning fire up its Avons. Jeremy Clarkson has a Lightning in his back garden!

After more than a quarter of a century as one of the RAF's air defence fighters, the English Electric Lightning ceased to be a frontline interceptor on 30 April 1988. Britain, once the workshop of the world, which designed and built innovative 'planes, trains and automobiles' for the Empire, et al, may no longer be the powerhouse it once was but our engineering heritage is second to none. Nostalgia is alive and well and Lightnings are without doubt the best of the 'Best of British'!

Martin W. Bowman,

BACKGROUND

Early in 1947 W.E.W. 'Teddy' Petter, chief design engineer at English Electric in Preston, received from the Ministry of Supply a study contract (Experimental Requirement ER 103) which called for a high-speed research aircraft capable of Mach 1.5. Companies such as Avro, Hawkers and SARO initiated design studies, but in the final analysis the delta-winged Fairey FD.2 and English Electric P.1 were deemed the most successful. Initial design studies for the P.1 began in 1948. Taking into consideration the work done by German aerodynamicists during the Second World War, the design team at English Electric decided on using highly swept-back wings and tailplane. The wing section had to be thin enough to reduce drag at high speed to a minimum, but also be capable of producing sufficient lift at low speed to give a good take off and landing performance. In mid-1949 Specification F.23/49 was issued and English Electric started work on two prototype P.1s and a structural test specimen. Petter's team utilised experience gained on the English

▼
F.2s and T.4s nearing completion on the production line at Samlesbury. (Aeroplane)

Did you know?

In 1960 English Electric Aviation was merged with Bristol, Vickers Armstrong (Aircraft) and Hunting Aircraft to form the British Aircraft Corporation (BAC).

WG760 being flown by English Electric's chief test pilot, Wing Commander Roland P. 'Bee' Beamont. The P.1A's leading edge chord-wise slot is very visible. (Charles E. Brown)

Electric A1 jet bomber (Canberra) and data from the Shorts S.B.5 research aircraft. Power was provided by two Armstrong Siddeley Sapphire AS-Sa 5s, each giving 8,100lb of thrust, considerably less than the eventual Rolls-Royce Avon 302s which provided 16,360lb of thrust per engine in

full reheat. The engines were 'stacked' one above and behind the other to double the thrust while increasing the frontal area by only 50 per cent over that of a single unit. The P.1's wings were swept at sixty degrees to minimise wave drag, with ailerons on the outer trailing-edge to the tips. A swept-back all-moving tailplane was mounted below the wing plane. The main undercarriage wheels retracted into the wings.

In 1950 Petter left English Electric to join Folland Aircraft and responsibility for the P.1 design and subsequent development passed to F.W. (later Sir 'Freddie') Page.

By spring 1954 WG760, the first prototype P.1, powered by two 7,500lb thrust Sapphires, was ready to fly. It took to the air for the first time at the A&AEE (Aircraft & Armament Experimental Establishment) Boscombe Down on 4 August 1954, flown by English Electric's chief test pilot, Wing Commander Roland P. 'Bee' Beamont, who reached Mach 0.85. On the third flight, on 11 August, Roland Beamont broke the sound barrier and WG760 became Britain's first truly supersonic jet, capable of exceeding Mach 1 in level flight. The second prototype, P.1A WG763, flew on 18 July 1955, and in September made its first public demonstration at the SBAC (Society of British Aircraft Companies) Farnborough show. The P.1A prototype differed from the P.1 in that it had two 30mm Aden cannon in the nose and American-style toe-brakes. WG760 and WG763 were subsequently re-designated P1.A, and the fighter project became P.1B. In 1954 three P.1B prototypes with 200 Series Rolls-Royce Avons and afterburning were ordered. Provision was made for AI23 (Airborne Intercept radar)

and two de Havilland Blue Jay (Firestreak) infrared self-guided active radar homing missiles. There were eventually four marks of Firestreak: Mk.I was fitted to high subsonic aircraft with an altitude of 55,000ft; Mk.II was fitted with a more sensitive nose; Mk.III for use by P.1 and Saro P.177 aircraft; and Mk.IV with full collision course variant

▼
P.1A WG760, which flew for the first time at the A&AEE Boscombe Down on 4 August 1954, being flown by Wing Commander 'Bee' Beamont, who reached Mach 0.85 on the first flight.

F.3 XP697, which flew for the first time on 18 July 1963 and became the F.6 prototype, flying for the first time on 17 April 1964. The first of sixty-two F.6 production models was issued to AFDS on 16 November 1965.

(which became Red Top). Production of Firestreak was undertaken by de Havilland's factory at Lostock from 1956, and about 2,500 missiles were manufactured up until 1969 when Red Top and Sky Flash succeeded it.

Lightning at the SBAC show at Farnborough in September 1959. (Ian Cadwallader)

Did you know?

On 5 January 1966 Flying Officer Derek Law of 56 Squadron suffered an engine flame-out and tried to eject, but the canopy jammed. Despite a successful belly-landing in a field near Woodbridge, Suffolk, he was killed when his ejection seat fired him through the branches of a tree.

A pre-series batch of twenty Lightning P.1Bs (plus three test airframes) followed the three P.1B prototypes. On 4 April 1957 the first prototype P.1B (XA847) exceeded Mach 1 without reheat on its first flight, in the hands of Roland Beamont.

DB (Development Batch) Lightning XG325 toting two Red Top drill rounds on the missile pylons. (BAe)

F.2 XN725 with over-wing tanks was later converted to the F.3 prototype. (BAe)

Exactly a year later the first of the pre-production batch of twenty P.1Bs was delivered. The first (XG307) flew on 3 April 1958. On 23 October the P.1B was flown at Farnborough. On 25 November XA847 became the first British aircraft to fly at Mach 2 and, on 6 January 1959, it exceeded Mach 2.

In November 1956 twenty production F.1 aircraft were ordered. These differed externally in having a central shock cone in the nose in place of the oval intake. Armament was two 30mm Aden cannon mounted at shoulder level aft of the cockpit. Alternative weapons packs consisting of additional guns or unguided air-to-air rockets

◀
Getting suited-up for a high altitude flight. (via Tony Aldridge)

▲
Warton test pilots, left to right: Don Knight, Desmond 'Dizzy' de Villiers, Peter Hillwood, Jimmy Dell and Roland Beamont. (BAe)

could be fitted in place of Firestreaks. The F.1 was extremely short-range, so a jettisonable ventral tank carrying an additional 2,000lb of fuel was fitted as standard. Even then the total fuel capacity was only 7,500lb, so although the Lightning could cruise

Did you know?

When on 4 April 1957 XA847, the first prototype P.1B, exceeded Mach 1 without reheat on its maiden flight, the Minister of Defence published his infamous *White Paper* forecasting the end of manned-combat aircraft (including a manned-supersonic bomber) and their replacement by ground-to-air missiles!

economically at altitude using 60lb of fuel a minute, with full reheat (or afterburner) its consumption increased tenfold to 600lb a minute.

When the first F.1 production example (XM134) flew on 3 November 1959 it was powered by two 11,250lb static thrust Avon RA.24R 210s, providing 14,430lb of static thrust in full reheat. The total thrust available, with full afterburner, was 29,000lb. It was not necessary to use reheat for take off. The initial rate of climb was in the order of 50,000ft per minute. Once airborne, the critical speeds were not much different from the Hunter, but the acceleration was much faster. Since the aircraft, fully loaded with fuel and weapons, weighed only 34,000lb, its

Did you know?

When in 1947-49 English Electric were invited to design two prototypes, a third airframe for static test and two 7g (gravity) research aircraft 'to investigate the practicality of supersonic speed for military aircraft', the company's previous experience of aircraft production had been limited to Hampden and Halifax bombers during the Second World War!

power-to-weight ratio was far better than any previous British fighter. In just ten years English Electric had recovered the ground lost during the late forties as a result of the government's moratorium on research into high-speed flight.

Three pre-series P.1Bs (XG334/335/336) entered service with AFDS (Air Fighting Squadron) at Coltishall, the first being delivered on 23 December 1959. Only the more experienced jet pilots (with 1,000 flying hours or more) were selected to fly the Lightning, and the initial training was accomplished with up to eleven hours in a flight simulator because the Lightning Conversion Flight had no Lightnings of its

◄
T.4 XM972 and others of the LCS (Lightning Conversion Squadron) at Middleton St George in 1961.

own. There was no T.4 dual Lightning until 1961, so the first flight was also a first solo. On 29 June 1960 XM165, one of nineteen production F.1s, was issued to 74 'Tiger' Squadron at Coltishall, which was destined to become the first operational squadron in Fighter Command to be equipped with the Lightning. Deliveries of the F.1, however,

◄ 56 Squadron personnel in Cyprus, 1964. (Brian Allchin)

▲ F.1A XM179 (right) and XM178 of 56 Squadron taking off from Wattisham in 1963. XM179 was lost in a collision near the station on 6 June 1963. (BAe)

➤ 92 Squadron's attractive royal blue and cobra-entwined tails. (Brian Allchin)

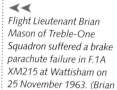

Flight Lieutenant Brian Mason of Treble-One Squadron suffered a brake parachute failure in F.1A XM215 at Wattisham on 25 November 1963. (Brian Allchin)

Ground crew winch a Red Top drill round onto the port missile pylon of a 23 Squadron F.6 at RAF Leuchars. (BAe)

Two F.6s of 5 Squadron,
their brake chutes
billowing, taxi in after
landing at Leconfield.
(Dick Bell)

XP750 of Treble-One Squadron. This Lightning was built originally as an F.3 and first flew in January 1964. (Dick Bell)

were slow, and by August 1960 only seven had arrived for 74 Squadron. 56 Squadron converted to the Lightning F.1 at Wattisham, Suffolk, in December 1960.

The F.1 had the necessary plumbing for in-flight refueling, with the provision for a detachable refuelling probe under the port wing, and it became the responsibility of 56 Squadron to pioneer flight refuelling for all the Lightning squadrons. Squadron Leader (later Group Captain) Dave Seward and his pilots began perfecting the art of air-to-air refuelling in 1962. At first they trained on USAF F-100Ds with Boeing KC-97s as tankers before air refuelling in earnest with RAF Vickers Valiant tankers. All F.1s were

F.1A XM179 of 56 Squadron was lost in a collision near RAF Wattisham on 6 June 1963. The pilot, Mike Cooke, managed to eject but was seriously injured and never flew again. (Brian Allchin)

Lightnings at sunset at RAF Coltishall in the 1960s. (Peter Symes)

F.1A XM173 of 56 Squadron taking on fuel from a Vickers Valiant in January 1964. (Brian Allchin)

➤➤
A pair of 56 Squadron's F.IAs about to begin in-flight refuelling from a Vickers Valiant. (Brian Allchin)

F.1 XM179 of 56 Squadron tanking from Vickers Valiant XD816. (via Dave Seward)

subsequently modified to F.1A, and 56 Squadron was the first to receive the F.1A (XM169), which first flew on 16 August 1960. In all, twenty-eight improved F.1A versions (and twenty T.4 versions of the F.1A) were produced. The 1A's two Rolls Royce Avons, with reheat, produced 11,250lb of thrust 'dry' and around 14,000lb 'wet'. Fuel capacity with the 250-gallon ventral tank installed was 1,020 gallons (although forty gallons of that was unusable). However, all fuel shown on the two fuel gauges was 'usable'. Weight was around fourteen tons with a full fuel load. Once the ventral tank was empty the power-to-weight ratio was better than 1lb of thrust to 1lb of weight. Fuel consumption at idle (31 per cent) was 156 gallons per hour per engine. At 100 per cent (maximum power), with reheat, it was 3,119 gallons per hour per engine.

Sortie time was normally around forty-five to fifty minutes. With reheat on, practice interceptions could be maintained for twenty to twenty-five minutes. From 0-250 knots, the Lightning would be at 5,000ft! Instead of two ten-channel VHF radios the F.1A was fitted with the latest UHF radio which had nineteen preset channels and the availability of nearly 2,000 manually-dialled frequencies. Another valuable addition was a rain-removal system: hot air tapped from the engines could be blown in front of the windscreen to keep it clear of precipitation. 111 Squadron at Wattisham began receiving the F.1A early in 1961, but, as they were delivered at the rate of one a week, it was mid-July before 'Treble One' (111) reached its full complement of twelve.

The Lightning presented a major challenge. It was the RAF's first supersonic,

night/all-weather interceptor. In speed alone it doubled the performance of the Hunter. But more than that, with its combination of AI23 (airborne interception radar) and Firestreak air-to-air guided weapons, the Lightning had a genuine interception capability against high-performance bomber aircraft. Opinion within Fighter Command was sharply divided as to the need for gun armament on modern fighters. Missile supporters claimed that only guided missiles would be effective in future air combat, while those who supported the gun insisted that it was still the best short-range, multi-shot weapon available. The Lightning was designed as a high-level, fast response interceptor because that was the perceived threat at the time. As a result the Lightning's guns pointed up by a few degrees, an angle which was exacerbated by the increased angle of attack if flying at a low air speed. The idea was that the Lightning would manoeuvre into a position astern of the target by using the information from the AI23 onboard radar. The aircraft would then close into gun range keeping below the target's slipstream. However, the actual threat during the service life of the Lightning was predominantly low-level, and if a low-level target had been engaged as previously described the Lightning would have hit the ground or sea long before achieving a firing position. But for the time being the main thrust of the Lightning weapons development was limited to the Firestreak. With the introduction of the Lightning, air defence was at last being given an appropriate degree of priority, which many fighter experts thought was long overdue.

Lightning F.1A on a reheat take off. (BAe)

In September 1960 Squadron Leader (later AVM) John F.G. Howe, a South African by birth, who had flown SAAF F-86 Sabres in the Korean War, led formation flypasts of four F.1s at the Farnborough Air Show. 74 Squadron became fully operational the following year, and a nine-ship formation was flown at the next Farnborough show in 1961. *Flight* reported:

> Nothing in the show exuded more sheer power than the three-second interval stream take off by the nine Lightnings of 74 Squadron, beating down the runway in a sustained blast of brown dust and stomach-shaking noise. As the rear machines were taking off, the leaders were climbing an invisible, vertical wall over Laffan's Plain. All were airborne in 35 seconds…

In 1962 the *Tigers* became the official Fighter Command aerobatic team. Later that same year the *Firebirds* of 56 Squadron were named the second of the official Fighter Command Lightning aerobatic display teams for the 1963 season. The team's name was derived from the squadron's *Phoenix rising from the ashes* emblem. Incredible as it now seems 56 Squadron were expected to continue day-to-day operations while at the same time working as the formation display team. Although the *Firebirds* began most of their displays with synchronised aerobatics from two sections of four or five aircraft, each show that summer of 1963 was opened by the full formation of nine with, sometimes, an extra solo performance thrown in. In September 1964 92 Squadron did the Farnborough air display with the

F.2. They were scrambled and did a reheat rotation take off. In 1965 the *Red Arrows* took over the mantle. The rest, as they say, is history. The first T.4 (P.11) side-by-side dual-controlled trainer version, based on the F.1A, flew on 15 July 1960. The Aden

Line up of 74 Squadron F.1s at RAF Coltishall in Norfolk. (BAe)

Did you know?

When in January 1965 92 Squadron's turn came to fly a detachment to Cyprus, the deployment coincided with the withdrawal from service of all Valiants after dangerous metal fatigue had been discovered in their airframes, so the Lightnings had to be 'puddle-jumped' to Cyprus via Germany, France and Sardinia!

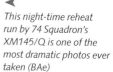
This night-time reheat run by 74 Squadron's XM145/Q is one of the most dramatic photos ever taken (BAe)

Prototype T.4 XL628, the first two-seater, which was flown on 6 May 1959, is seen here with P.1B XG331 during a test flight from Warton. XL628 was lost over the Irish Sea on 1 October 1959. (BAe)

▲
The Firebirds in formation over Wattisham. (Brian Allchin)

➤
56 Squadron – the Firebirds – lined up at Wattisham. (MoD)

Squadron Leader Dave Seward, CO of 56 Squadron. (via Edwin Carter)

T.4 XM997 of 226 OCU from RAF Coltishall over the North Sea in September 1965. (Jimmy Jewell)

F.1A XM216, T.4 XM997 and T.5 XS419 of 226 OCU at Coltishall in 1971. (BAe)

cannon was removed, but two Firestreak missiles were normally carried. A total of twenty T.4s were built. Two of them were later converted to T.5 standard, while British Aircraft Corporation (BAC) purchased two for export as T.54s to Saudi Arabia.

The T.5 was a two-seat version based on the F.3A, and a total of twenty-two production T.5s were built for the RAF. The T.5 prototype (XM967, a converted T.4) first flew on 29 March 1962 at Filton, Bristol. The first production T.5 (XS417) flew on 17 July 1964 and the first examples

entered service with 226 OCU at Coltishall in April 1965. It is now difficult to believe, but the controls for the T.4 and T.5 differed substantially. All military fast jets are controlled by a stick in the right-hand and throttle(s) in the left; the trainer versions are generally configured in the same fashion, as, indeed, was the T.4. However, the T.5 was

different. For the right seat occupant the throttles were mounted on the right-hand side of the cramped side-by-side cockpit, and the flying controls were operated by a stick with the left hand. This arrangement could cause some coordination problems during certain phases of flight, particularly in formation flying and landing.

Strike Command's air defence of the UK in 1980 consisted of two Lightning and five Phantom squadrons as against Fighter Command's thirty-three Hurricane and Spitfire squadrons at the beginning of the Battle of Britain in 1940. QRA, or Quick Reaction Alert, was the Lightning's *raison d'etre*. RAF Fighter (later Strike) Command stationed Lightnings and later Lightnings and Phantoms on a special 'ready' pan, armed and ready to go at a few minutes' notice. The pilots' task was to intercept, supersonically, any aircraft approaching the UK without a flight plan or who crossed into the air defence zone without warning and, if ordered, shoot them down with missiles and cannon fire. In the UK this permanent state of high readiness was called QRA, while in Germany it was known as Battle Flight. In the UK this allowed ten minutes

after notice, while in Germany five minutes were allowed. Air and ground crew waited in their ready rooms twenty-four hours a day, 365 days a year. The Q Shed, a self-contained unit which housed both air and ground crew in an adjacent bungalow,

➤

An 11 Squadron F.6 on QRA in the Q Shed in the 1980s. (Malcolm English)

48

MoD publicity photo of two Lightning pilots on QRA running to their Lightning's. (MoD)

Did you know?

Squadron commanders did not do normal QRA, but, generally speaking, they did Christmas Day and Boxing Day duty, especially so on Christmas Day 1962 when the Russians, who could be 'bloody minded', put up a stream of Bears and the odd Bison round the North Cape

A Lightning shadowing a Soviet Bear over the North Sea in July 1968. (Bruce Hopkins)

Did you know?

From 1966 onwards interception of Soviet Bears over the North Sea became more frequent, right around the clock. International rules of the air obliged Lightning pilots to approach on the left. It was also a matter of courtesy for the Soviet pilots to sit in the left-hand seats of their cockpits, making it easier to exchange waves and smiles!

was built away from the airfield hangars, adjacent to the main runway, in order to minimise aircraft taxiing time prior to take off. Ground crew could stay for a week at a time, all living in accommodation just a few feet from their aircraft. It was a popular duty because a Lightning pilot was almost certain to get a training scramble during

Did you know?

Diana Barnato-Walker MBE, a legendary Air Transport Auxiliary pilot, became the first British woman to qualify as a member of the '1,000mph Club' (otherwise known as the 'Ten Ton Club') on 26 August 1963. Accompanied by Squadron Leader Ken Goodwin, she clocked Mach 1.65 (1,262mph), which for a short time was the unofficial women's speed record. Diana was billed in the *Sunday Express* as Britain's fastest mum!

each period, and always had the next day off. The reason for the frequent training scrambles was that five minutes really was not very long to run to a Lightning, climb the ladder, strap in, start engines, taxi to the runway and take off. If the pilots were asleep when the 'scramble' bell sounded the time allowed was even tighter.

Once an alert sounded the two pilots would belt for their transport and drive across to the pan where, strapped in, they were ready to be airborne within two minutes. Ground crew supplied external power to the Lightnings during these waiting periods, and the pilots got their briefing via a plug-in telebrief direct from the relevant operations room. Many of the Lightning alerts were practices – intruders simulated by Canberras from RAF Germany – but there were also 'quite a few' visitors from Russia, some of them long-

range maritime flights from the far north, which flew past Norway and turned over the Shetlands. Visual identification of strange targets was practiced by the Lightning pilots, approaching the intruder from behind and at 300 yards range, identifying them visually. At night this had to be done in whatever light was available. On all occasions a radar lock-on had to be achieved. Aircraft that were put up against the QRA force included Canberras, Phantoms, Buccaneers and Sea Vixens. All Lightning pilots underwent an intensive aircraft recognition course at the OTU (Operational Training Unit) and, after arriving on the squadron, they were kept in practice by continuous refresher training, both simulated and live. Some visitors clearly tested the readiness of the QRA force, playing 'cat and mouse' with the Lightnings, flying close enough to wake up pilots and then

turning away before they were scrambled. Others listened for the signatures of NATO ECM devices, and there were electronic-

intelligence gatherers who flew around listening-in to radio and radar frequencies. There were even some practice bombing

At Lyneham on 22 July 1966 forty-year-old Wing Commander Walter 'Taffy' Holden, CO of 33 MU, went for an unscheduled trip in a Lightning. While carrying out ground runs, XM135 jumped the chocks, locked in reheat, and took off! Holden, who had never flown a jet aircraft before, was not wearing a helmet and the canopy had been removed prior to the taxi tests, yet he remained airborne for twelve minutes and managed to land safely at the second attempt! XM135 is now in the IWM collection at Duxford.

runs. Whatever the intruders were doing, the Lightnings intercepted, identified and accompanied them out of the area, armed with cameras and live missiles. Nobody has ever refused to go.

Normally the Lightnings on QRA operated with the local air defence radar network, which would vector the interceptors onto a target until the Ferranti Airpass AI23B radar had picked them up. The AI23B was a pilot-interpreted system, which meant that the pilot must position himself within brackets which were displayed in order to make an effective missile firing. To do this he could fly a computed flight path, also displayed, or position himself manually. The technique in an attack was to approach the target either very high or very low so that the intruder could easily be seen without the Lightning itself being spotted. For very high-level attacks the technique was to accelerate to supersonic speed near the tropopause and then climb at attack speed to the height required. The Lightning was still able to climb quicker and accelerate to supersonic speeds faster than the Phantom, and was therefore ideal for the QRA role. The Lightning's greatest attribute was said to be its handling qualities. It was highly maneuverable, particularly in the transonic bands.

Did you know?
On 23 May 1967 Wing Commander Mick Swiney led twenty-five Lightnings and two Spitfires of the Battle of Britain Memorial Flight – all from RAF Coltishall – over Norwich to mark twenty-seven years of RAF association with this fine city.

The Handley Page Victor in-flight refuelling crews were a closely-knit family who took great pride in their exclusive role, unashamedly referring to themselves as the 'Tanker Trash'. Fuel, or a lack of it, was always a problem for the Lightnings, especially when they were called upon to fulfill defence commitments in the Far East. Various solutions were tried, not least 260 gallon over-wing fuel tanks, nicknamed 'overburgers', which prompted the retort that only the British could defy the laws of gravity and prevent fuel from flowing downwards! Tanking was an essential part of Lightning operations and 'prods and bracket' training was intensive. Exercise *Forthright 22/23* to Cyprus, in August 1965, was the first occasion when the Victor tanker was used for operational overseas deployment, with four of 74 Squadron's Lightning F.3s being flown from Leuchars via Wattisham to Akrotiri. That October the F.3s in Cyprus were air-refuelled all the way to Tehran and back by Victor tankers. In 1966 56 Squadron were tanked to Malta and back. In February 1967 Exercise *Forthright 59/60* saw Lightning F.3s flying non-stop to Akrotiri and F.6s returning to the UK, refuelled throughout by Victor tankers. In April 56 Squadron's Lightnings flew to Cyprus, carrying out six in-flight refuellings for the fighter versions and ten for the two-seat T-birds. In-flight refuelling from Victors also became a feature of QRA missions in the UK.

In June 1967 seventeen Victor tankers refuelled 74 'Tiger' Squadron's thirteen F.6 Lightnings, which flew to Tengah, Singapore, in Operation *Hydraulic*, the longest and largest in-flight refuelling operation hitherto

No.74 Tiger Squadron badge. (Author)

flown. All the Lightnings reached Tengah safely, staging through Akrotiri, Masirah and Gan. The Lightnings remained at Tengah for four years, and during this time three 2,000-mile deployments were made to Australia, non-stop, using Victor tankers, the major one being Exercise *Town House 16-26* in June 1969.

Flight Lieutenant Roger Pope in F.6 XS897/K comes up close to Flight Lieutenant Dave Roome in F.6 XR773/F during the 74 Squadron flight from Tengah to Gan on 6 September 1971. (Group Captain D. Roome)

Remarkable view of a 74 Squadron Lightning through the periscope of a Victor tanker during an air-to-air refuelling ferry flight from Tengah to Cyprus in September 1971. (Jimmy Jewell)

Did you know?

In June 1967 thirteen of 74 Squadron's F.6s
transferred from the UK to Tengah, Singapore,
in Operation *Hydraulic*, the longest and largest
in-flight refuelling operation hitherto flown,
staging through Akrotiri, Masirah and Gan,
using seventeen Victor tankers from Marham,
for a four-year tour of duty.

74 Squadron's Lightnings at Tengah. (Dave Roome)

74 Squadron Lightning at Tengah. (John Hale)

'A' Flight Detachment, 74 Squadron at RAAF Butterworth, Malaya, in February 1968. (Jimmy Jewell)

XR768/A of 74 Squadron air-to-air refuelling with a Victor tanker. (MoD)

►►

F.3 refuelling from the centreline tank of a Victor K.1A in 1972. (Dick Bell)

In the tropics, where the tropopause is in the order of 55,000ft, the Lightning could achieve heights above 85,000ft. The tropopause is the height at which the stratosphere begins. It varies with latitude and season, but can be taken as approximately 36,000ft, above which the temperature remains constant. On at least

XP756/E of 29 Squadron with a Victor tanker. (Dick Bell)

Did you know?

On 28 August 1968, in the first ever Lightning crossing of the Atlantic, two F.6s of 23 Squadron at RAF Leuchars, flown by the CO, Squadron Leader Ed Durham, and Flight Lieutenant Geoff Brindle, made the non-stop, air-refuelled, seven-hours and twenty-minutes flight to Goose Bay, Canada, to appear in the International Exhibition at Toronto.

F.3 XP756/E of 29 Squadron moves in to refuel from Victor K.1A XH649 of 57 Squadron over the Alps during an exchange exercise to Grosseto, Italy, in July 1968. (Dick Bell)

F.3s of 29 Squadron tanking from a Victor of 55 Squadron. (MoD)

T.5 XS458 of 226 OCU and a Victor tanker in formation. (Dick Bell)

one occasion a 74 'Tiger' Squadron pilot climbed initially to 50,000ft, which was the subsonic service ceiling of the aircraft, and there accelerated to Mach 2 to begin a zoom climb, then levelled off at 65,000ft and reached Mach 2.2 before once again flying the same zoom profile, until eventually topping out 200ft short of 88,000ft!

On 29 November 1967 an 11 Squadron Lightning established a record of eight-and-a-half-hours flying, being refuelled five times and covering 5,000 miles. The withdrawal of British forces from the Far East involved a rapid reinforcement commitment. In May 1968 four F.6 Lightnings of 5 Squadron at Leconfield flew non-stop from Binbrook to Bahrain in eight hours, refuelled along the 4,000-mile route by Victor tankers. The rapid reinforcement commitment continued, and on 6 January

1969 Exercise *Piscator*, the biggest in-flight refuelling exercise so far mounted by the RAF, took place when ten Lightning F.6s of 11 Squadron were deployed to Tengah, staging through Muharraq and Gan and back, covering a total distance of 18,500 miles. Victors of 55, 57 and 214 Squadrons refuelled each Lightning thirteen times. Throughout the two-way journey 228 individual refuelling contacts were made, during which 166,000 imperial gallons (754,630 litres) of fuel were transferred.

During Christmas 1969 Exercise *Ultimacy* involved ten F.6s of 5 Squadron flying to Tengah for joint air-defence exercises in Singapore. The first Lightnings began leaving Binbrook before dawn on a foggy 8 December morning. At 0345 hours they made their first rendezvous with their Victor tankers over East Anglia in the

In 1968 a fiberglass Guinness toucan stolen from a Newcastle public house was flown to 1,000mph membership and became a jealously guarded trophy. At a great Guinness party the disappearance of the Park Royal tower clock caused a major Guinness sense of humour failure, and further hospitality to the Lightning fraternity ceased. Another highly sought after trophy was the pilot head tube on the Lightning, which made an ideal lamp standard in quarters!

Ten-Ton ties, one with the Mach symbol, and the other with the 'flying toucan'.

dark. Then it was on across France and the Mediterranean for a rendezvous with more Victors from Cyprus. They then continued eastwards, crossing Muscat and Oman on their way to Masirah, the overnight stop. Next day a pre-dawn take off saw the Lightnings away on the last leg of their trip, heading south-east across 4,000 miles of ocean to Gan where they rendezvoused with more Victors before turning due east for Sumatra. Some of 74 Squadron's Lightnings were in need of a major overhaul, so pairs of Lightnings left for the UK, again being refuelled by Victors between stopovers at Masirah and Akrotiri.

Did you know?

By 1968 the 'Ten-Ton Club' included well over 900 members, from Royal patronage's such as King Hussein of Jordan and the Shah of Iran to people of more humble origins. On 27 February Group Captain Mike Hobson, the RAF Coltishall station commander, flew Mr Hastings of the Royal Observer Corps at 1,066mph!

X N723, the F.2 prototype, first flew on 11 July 1961, and forty-four were built to F.2 production standard, the first being delivered to AFDS at Binbrook on 4 November 1962. One F.2 was converted to F.3 standard, one to F.3A, and five became F.52s for service with the RSAF. Externally, the F.2 looked similar to the F.1A, but its Avon 210 engines were now fully variable afterburning instead of four-stage. F.2s were configured with four 30mm Aden cannon, the lower guns displacing the two Firestreaks. Additionally, F.2s also had an improved cockpit layout, an automatic flight control system, all-weather navigational aids and liquid oxygen (LOX). The F.2As were F.2s rebuilt to incorporate some F.6 features such as kinked and cambered wings, square-cut fins which provided a greater area and an enlarged ventral fuel tank, two Aden cannon in the upper nose and two AAMs (Air-To-Air Missiles).

◄ Lightning going into reheat. (via Tony Aldridge)

◄ F.3s of Treble-One Squadron in formation. (MoD)

On 17 December 1962 19 Squadron at RAF Leconfield became the first operational RAF squadron to receive the Lightning F.2. In the summer of 1963 the Leconfield Wing became fully operational on the F.2, while 19 Squadron were joined by the F.2s of 92 Squadron. On 23 September 1965, 19 Squadron's dozen F.2s moved to

This 1965 shot shows F.2 XN779/G of 19 Squadron nearest the camera followed by F.3 XP746/K of 56 Squadron, F.3 XP739/H of Treble-One Squadron and F.2 XN783/A of 92 Squadron. (BAe)

Gütersloh, eighty miles from the East German border, to begin patrolling the air identification zone, together with F.2As of 92 Squadron at Geilenkirchen from the end of December 1965. The role increasingly saw the F.2s and F.2As being used in low-level interception. Beginning in January 1968, thirty-one of the F.2s still

serving with 19 and 92 Squadrons in RAF Germany were modified to F.2A standard to incorporate some of the latter's features. These included the larger 610 gallon ventral tank in place of the earlier 250 imperial gallon jettisonable tank, the square-cut tail fin and cranked and cambered wing, which gave better control throughout the speed

Did you know?

Victor floodlights, which lit up the under-surface of the tanker's wings, ruined night vision and blinded Lightning pilots as they tanked at night, so they were turned off, leaving just the tanker's navigation lights and the small triangles of blue lights on the basket. Tanking in the dark was that much easier because they could not see and were therefore not distracted by the refuelling probe while trying to engage the basket.

▲
92 Squadron's Lightnings in a weak formation. (Tony Aldridge)

➤
F.3 XP743/B of 29 Squadron in 1972. (BAe)

F.2A XN781/B of 19 Squadron at RAF Leconfield in 1968, being prepared for the delivery flight to Gütersloh following a major service by 60 MU. (Dick Bell)

range, while retaining the smaller Avon engines and the upper Aden cannon. The last F.2A for RAF Germany was delivered to 92 Squadron on 5 July 1970.

The F.3 was introduced in 1962. It was powered by two 12,690lb dry thrust Avon 501 engines (16,360lb in reheat) and had an improved AI23b fire control radar as well

as a larger, squared off-fin. Unlike the earlier models, which were cleared to Mach 1.7, F.3s were cleared to Mach 2. Provisions were made for two jettisonable over-wing tanks (the long undercarriage retracted outwards making it impossible to put them under the wing) and Red Top missiles in place of the Firestreak (which permitted head-on attacks

on supersonic targets). However, the extra circuitry for the radar, plus the liquid oxygen system, meant the Aden cannon had to be deleted. The first prototype F.3 (XP693) flew on 16 June 1962, and the first production versions entered service with the Central Fighter Establishment (CFE) at Binbrook in January 1964. In April 74 Squadron at Leuchars became the first RAF squadron to receive the F.3 when it began replacing its F.1s. On 18 August, 23 Squadron, also at Leuchars, began replacing its Javelins with the F.3, and was fully operational by early 1965. At Wattisham, 56 and Treble-One Squadrons began receiving the F.3 in late 1964, their F.1As being transferred to other units. A total of seventy F.3s were built, while sixteen F.3As (interim F.6s) were produced. All the F.3As and nine F.3s were converted to F.6, the first of these flying on 17 April 1964.

Flight Lieutenant Tony Aldridge of 23 Squadron maintains formation with F.3 XP763/M on take off from Leuchars in July 1965. (via Tony Aldridge)

Did you know?

West German F-104G Starfighters suffered a higher attrition than the RAF Lightnings, but the latter's percentage losses were higher! It was said that to acquire a Starfighter one bought a plot of land and waited, and to obtain a Lightning you 'bought a piece of North Sea and waited'! The Starfighter had, eventually, the same straight-line top speeds, but could never match the Lightning's rate of turn at any speed.

With their more powerful engines and small ventral tank, both the F.3 and the T.5 were very tight on fuel. The British Aircraft Corporation identified the F.6 as the solution. This mark, originally known as the F.3A or the 'interim F.6', was essentially an F.3 with increased internal fuel tankage and other long-range modifications, chief of which was the cambered and kinked leading edge wing, which allowed operation at greater weights. The 610-gallon ventral tank combined with the low subsonic drag

➤

F.3 XR725/A of 23 Squadron, which Squadron Leader Ed Durham flew non-stop to Goose Bay, Canada, on 27 August 1968. (Group Captain Durham)

➤➤

F.6 XS920/F of 11 Squadron with over-wing tanks. (Dick Bell)

*F.6 XP693 of 56 Squadron
at RAF Wattisham on
3 July 1992, being used as
a chase plane for Tornado
F.2 and F.3 development.*

*F.6 XS931/G of 11
Squadron. (Dick Bell)*

of the 'new' leading edge (first flown in 1956) increased the fuel load to 10,608lb (as carried by the F.6) or about 15,000lb with 260-gallon over-wing ferry tanks. This was more than double that of the early Lightnings, which managed just 497lb or 622 gallons. The F.6 prototype (XP697) flew for the first time on 17 April 1964.

The first of sixty-two F.6 production models was issued to AFDS on 16 November 1965. On 10 December the F.6 entered squadron service with 5 Squadron at Binbrook. In September 1966 74 'Tiger' Squadron began converting to the F.6 from the F.3, and by the beginning of 1968, 23 Squadron, also at Leuchars, was fully equipped. On 1 April

1967, 11 Squadron re-formed at Leuchars with the F.6. On 1 May, 29 Squadron re-formed at Wattisham to become the last RAF squadron to equip with the Lightning (F.3s, mostly from 74 and 23 Squadrons).

On 25 August 1967 the thirty-eighth and final F.6 was delivered to the RAF. Total

F.6s of 23 Squadron in 1968. (BAe)

F.6 XS936/B of 23 Squadron. (BAe)

Did you know?

On 29 February 1968 nineteen-year-old WAAF Pilot Officer Vivienne Whyer at RAF Coltishall became the 1,000th member of the 'Ten Ton Club' when Group Captain Mike Hobson flew her at 1,000mph+ in a T.4, though only one engine would go to reheat.

Lightning production reached 339, with the last F.3 being delivered on 16 January 1968. In 1970 a decision was taken to install two Aden guns in the front of the ventral tank of the F.6s (though the F.3 remained without the guns). Beginning in 1971, the RAF Lightning squadrons began to disband one by one. First to go

98

◄◄
*F.6 of 19 Squadron of RAF
Germany at Gütersloh in
1975. (MoD)*

◄
*F.6 XR755/J of
11 Squadron in 1976.
(Tony Paxton)*

Did you know?

The Lightning always flew with two missile 'bodies' fitted, a weighted drill round on the port side and an acquisition on the starboard. It was always this way round to protect the glass seeker-head on the missile from being damaged by the access ladder when it was being fitted and removed.

was 74 Squadron, which disbanded at Tengah on 25 August 1971. All the 'Tigers' remaining F.6s were flown the 6,000-mile, thirteen-hour trip to Akrotiri, Cyprus, from 2 September, staging through Gan and Muharraq and completing seven air-to-air refuellings with Victor tankers, for transfer to 56 Squadron. Demonstrating the rapid deployment made possible by in-flight refuelling, in 1974 six Lightning F.6s were sent to Cyprus when a Greek-led coup by the Cyprus National Guard overthrew President Makarios. Treble-One Squadron disbanded at Wattisham on 30 September 1974 for conversion to Phantoms. Also in September, 226 OCU disbanded, then, on 31 December, 29 Squadron disbanded at Wattisham, re-forming as a Phantom squadron in 1975. On 31 October 1975, 23 Squadron was disbanded, being replaced

in the QRA role at Leuchars by Treble-One's FGR.2s. 56 Squadron formed using Phantoms on 22 March 1976. The two RAF Germany squadrons, 19 and 92, disbanded on 31 December 1976 and 31 March 1977 respectively, both units re-forming at Wildenrath early in 1977 using Phantoms. 74 Squadron re-formed as a Phantom squadron at Wattisham in 1984.

What is not generally known is that, of the 339 Lightnings built, no less than 109 were lost or written off during their service life. Many were lost to fuel or hydraulic leak-related fires, in what became known in the 1970s as 'LFS' or 'Lightning Fire Syndrome'. Between 1959 and 1969 forty-two Lightnings were lost. A fire-integrity programme was begun in 1968 which introduced modifications to the Lightning. In 1969 only one Lightning was lost, but in

F.6 XS417/DZ of the LTF at RAF Binbrook in the late 1980s.

Did you know?

AVPIN (isopropylnitrate starter fuel) was used to fire up the Lightning's Avons, the pilot raising and waggling an index finger to signal engine start. AVPIN pumps whined and a pitched scream assaulted the eardrums as the AVPIN ignited and spun the engine up to speed for ignition. After about five seconds the starter kicked out and the engine ignited and became self-sustaining. Starter fires were not uncommon.

1970 nine were written off. The worst year for Lightning losses was 1971, with thirteen destroyed. Eight more were written off in 1972. Despite the fire integrity programme, most of the losses in 1971 were due to fuel leak-related fires. On the other hand, fuel-related fires had caused none of the eight Lightnings lost in 1972.

Between 1973 and mid-1988, when the last Lightning was retired from frontline service, no more than five Lightnings were lost in any year. LTF (Lightning Training

Flight) disbanded at Binbrook on 1 August 1987, though 5 and 11 Squadrons operated some of their Lightnings for some months after that. 5 Squadron proved the longest operator of the Lightning, finally disbanding at Binbrook on 31 December 1987, re-forming as a Tornado F.3 unit at Coningsby on 1 May 1988. 11 Squadron was the last Lightning squadron to disband, on 30 April 1988, also re-forming as a Tornado F.3 unit at Leeming on 1 November 1988. Squadron Leader John Aldington had the distinction of making the final RAF Lightning flight when he delivered one of three aircraft to RAF Cranfield on 30 June 1988, thirty-four years after the P.1 first flew.

Did you know?

On 13 February 1980 Flight Lieutenant John 'Fynesy' Fynes of 5 Squadron, the last ever Lightning display pilot, suffered disorientation causing the aircraft to dive at Mach 1.3, producing 13.5 G, which severely overstressed the airframe causing the wings to crack, fuel to leak and the undercarriage mounting bracket to damage. Fynsey safely recovered to Binbrook where XS898 was declared Cat.3, stripped-down and repaired with reinforcing boilerplates!

In 1962-63 it became clear that the Saudi air defence system would have to be brought up to date. In July 1964 Wing Commander Jimmy Dell demonstrated a Lightning F.2 in Riyadh, and the Saudis were so impressed that a military mission was sent to Britain to discuss the British tender. Agreements were reached for thirty-four F.53/T.55 Lightnings for the RSAF (Royal Saudi Air Force), along with other British military equipment. The F.53 was the export version of the F.6, capable of carrying a wide range of ordnance including two Firestreak or two Red Top, 48 x 2in rockets in place of the missile pack and two 1,000lb HE bombs and thirty-six 84mm SNEB (Societé Nouvelle des Etablissments Edgar Brant) rockets in two Matra Type 155 launchers, either from over-wing or under-wing pylon hard points. In an attempt to prevent continued Yemeni incursions, the delivery of the Saudi Lightnings was preceded, in June 1966, by the arrival of five F.2s, urgently converted to F.52 standards for service with the RSAF. These, along with two ex-RAF T.4s which were

Royal Saudi Air Force T-Birds 55-712/B and 55-714/D at RAF Coltishall, Norfolk, in 1968. (Graham Mitchell)

➤
Royal Saudi Air Force T-Bird 55-714/D at RAF Coltishall, Norfolk, in 1968.

re-designed T.54s, were delivered to Saudi Arabia in Operation *Magic Carpet*, with ex-RAF pilots delivering them.

Between September 1966 and May 1970 three of the five F.52s were written off in crashes.

The first Lightning for the RSAF flew on 1 December 1966, and the first Saudi pilot to convert to the Lightning completed his training in June 1967. In December that same year the first Lightning delivery to Saudi Arabia took place. On 1 July 1968 F.53s, delivered by RAF and BAC pilots in Operation *Magic Palm*, began to arrive

◄
F.53 Lightnings of the Royal Saudi Air Force taking off from Jeddah. (BAe)

in Saudi Arabia. No.6 Squadron RSAF had been formed in 1967 from a group of Hunters and F.52 Lightnings, which were used in air defence until the arrival of the F.53s. The Lightning Flight was declared operational in November 1966. A Canberra was used to tow targets for firing practice. Joint exercises aimed at the air defence of the Eastern Sector were carried out. Two more Lightning squadrons – Nos 2 and 13 – were formed, and, what with the arrival of F.53s to 6 Squadron, F.53s carried out the entire defense of the southern zone during 1974-78.

In December 1968 Kuwait Air Force took delivery of the first of twelve F.53/T.55s.

In 1969 Saudi Arabia first used its F.53s in offensive action on ground strikes against border positions in Yemen. That same year 226 OCU at Coltishall was given the Saudi training commitment with four Saudi T.55s (a total of eight T.55s, the export version of the T.5, were built; six for the Royal Saudi Air Force and two for Kuwait).

With the arrival of the F-15 Eagle in 1981 Lightning operations began to diminish and the Lightnings were redistributed. No.2 Squadron RSAF was the last Saudi squadron to operate the Lightning, on 22 January 1986. Kuwait Air Force operated its F.53Ks and the two T.55Ks until 1977, when French Mirage F.1Ks replaced them.

Royal Saudi Air Force T.54 54-651 pulls in to air refuel in 1966. This Lightning was written off in 1970 after a starter fire at Khamis.

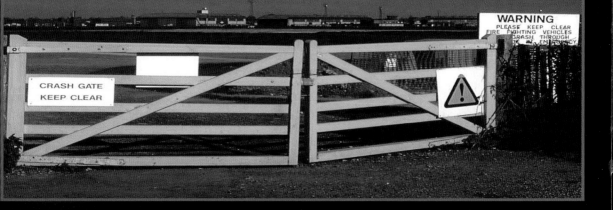

Airfields too have their entrances and exits
Where high drama can be enacted in starts and fits
Lightnings frequently taking off and landing
And for months, emergency vehicles are standing
Meticulously checked with crews perfect at crash-drill
Highly polished machines like showroom pieces until
A simple landing or take off gone wrong; no time to wait
The entrance or exit urgently required is that Yellow Gate.

Jasper Miles

CRASH GATE
KEEP CLEAR

WARNING
PLEASE KEEP CLEAR
FIRE FIGHTING VEHICLES
CRASH THROUGH
IN EMERGENCY

SPECIFICATIONS

Model	Span	Length	Height	Wing Area	Power Plant	Empty Weight	Loaded Weight	Max Speed	Service Ceiling	Armament
P.1A	34ft 10in	49ft 8in	17ft 3in	458.5	Armstrong Siddeley Sapphire 5	22,221lb	27,077lb	Mach 1.53 (1011 mph) @36,000 ft	55,000ft	2 x 30mm Aden cannon
P.1B	34ft 10in	55ft 3in	19ft 5in	458.5	RR Avon 200R	24,816lb	31,831lb	Mach 2.1 (1,390mph) @36,000ft	55,000ft	2 x 30mm Aden cannon
F.1	34ft 10in	55ft 3in	19ft 7in	458.5	RR Avon 200R	25,753lb	u/k	Mach 2.3 (1,500mph) @36,000ft	60,000ft	4 x 30mm Aden cannon or 2 x Firestreak AAM + 2 x 30mm cannon
F.1A	34ft 10in	55ft 3in	19ft 7in	458.5	RR Avon 210R	25,757lb	u/k	Mach 2.3 (1,500mph) @36,000ft	60,000ft	4 x 30mm Aden cannon or 2 x Firestreak AAM + 2 x 30mm cannon
F.2	34ft 10in	55ft 3in	19ft 7in	458.5	RR Avon 210R	27,000lb	u/k	Mach 2.3 (1,500mph) @36,000ft	60,000ft	4 x 30mm Aden cannon or 2 x Firestreak AAM + 2 x 30mm cannon

Model	Span	Length	Height	Wing Area	Power Plant	Empty Weight	Loaded Weight	Max Speed	Service Ceiling	Armament
F.2A	34ft 10in	55ft 3in	19ft 7in	458.5	RR Avon 2110R	27,500lb	u/k	Mach 2.3 (1,500mph) @36,000ft	60,000ft+	4 x 30mm Aden cannon or 2 x Firestreak AAM + 2 x 30mm cannon
F.3	34ft 10in	55ft 3in	19ft 7in	458.5	RR Avon 3010R	26,905lb	u/k	Mach 2.3 (1,500mph) @36,000ft	60,000ft+	4 x 30mm Aden cannon or 2 x 30mm cannon
F.3A	34ft 10in	55ft 3in	19ft 7in	458.5	RR Avon 301R	28,041lb	41,700lb	Mach 2.3 (1,500mph) @36,000ft	60,000ft+	2 x Firestreak AAM or 2 x Red Top AAM
T.4	34ft 10in	55ft 3in	19ft 7in	458.5	RR Avon 210R	27,000lb	u/k	Mach 2.3 (1,500mph) @36,000ft	60,000ft+	2 x Firestreak AAM
T.5	34ft 10in	55ft 3in	19ft 7in	458.5	RR Avon 301R	27,000lb	u/k	Mach 2.3 (1,500mph) @36,000ft	60,000ft+	2 x Firestreak AAM or 2 x Red Top AAM

Model	Span	Length	Height	Wing Area	Power Plant	Empty Weight	Loaded Weight	Max Speed	Service Ceiling	Armament
F.6	34ft 10in	55ft 3in	19ft 7in	458.5	RR Avon 301R	28,041lb	u/k	Mach 2.3 (1,500mph) @36,000ft	60,000ft+	2 x Firestreak AAM or 2 x Red Top AAM + 2 x 30mm Aden cannon in ventral tank, 48 x 2in rockets in place of missiles
F.53	34ft 10in	55ft 3in	19ft 7in	458.5	RR Avon 301	28,041lb	u/k	Mach 2.3 (1,500mph) @36,000ft	60,000ft+	As F.6 + 2 x 1,000lb bombs, 4 SNEB Matra rocket packs and Vinten camera recce pack.
T.55	34ft 10in	55ft 3in	19ft 7in	458.5	RR Avon 301	28,041lb	u/k	Mach 2.3 (1,500mph) @36,000ft	60,000ft+	2 x Firestreak AAM or 2 x Red Top AAM

MILESTONES

1947
English Electric receives study contract calling for a high-speed research aircraft capable of Mach 1.5.

1949
Specification F.23/49 issued for two prototype P.1s and a structural test specimen.

1950
W.E.W. 'Teddy' Petter, chief design engineer, leaves English Electric to join Folland Aircraft. Responsibility for the P.1 design and subsequent development passes to F.W. (later Sir 'Freddie') Page.

4 August 1954
First prototype P.1 reaches Mach 0.85 on the first flight.

11 August 1954
On the third flight WG760 and Roland Beamont break the sound barrier.

18 July 1955
P.1A WG763, the second prototype, flies.

September 1955
WG763 makes the first public demonstration at SBAC Farnborough.

November 1956
Twenty production F.1 aircraft ordered.

4 April 1957
XA847, the first prototype P.1B, exceeds Mach 1 without reheat on its first flight.

3 April 1958
The first of twenty pre-production P.1Bs (XG307) flies.

25 November 1958
XA847 becomes the first British aircraft to fly at Mach 2.

6 January 1959
XA847 exceeds Mach 2.

Did you know?
The thirty-four Lightnings acquired by Saudi Arabia were preceded in June 1966 by seven ex-RAF single- and two-seat Lightnings, using ex-RAF pilots to fly them, under a programme codenamed *Magic Carpet*. In 1968 *Magic Palm*, the second phase of the Saudi delivery programme, was begun

3 November 1959

First F.1 production example (XM134) flies.

23 December 1959

Three pre-series P.1Bs enter service with AFDS (Air Fighting Squadron) at Coltishall.

1960

English Electric Aviation merge with Bristol, Vickers Armstrong (Aircraft) and Hunting Aircraft, to form the British Aircraft Corporation (BAC).

29 June 1960

XM165, the first of nineteen production F.1s, is issued to 74 'Tiger' Squadron at Coltishall.

15 July 1960

The first T.4 (P.11) dual-controlled trainer version of the F.1A flies.

16 August 1960

F.1A (XM169) flies for first time.

Did you know?

A continuing problem with the Lightning concerned fuel and hydraulic fires. The two engines, No.2 mounted above and No.1 behind the missile pack, had long jet pipes close to the external skin.

December 1960
56 Squadron begins conversion to the Lightning F.1 at Wattisham, Suffolk.

11 July 1961
F.2 prototype (XN723) flies.

1961
74 Squadron becomes fully operational and a nine-ship formation is flown at Farnborough 1961.

March 1961
Treble-One Squadron at Wattisham receives all of its complement of F.1As.

1962
The Firebirds of 56 Squadron are named the official Fighter Command Lightning aerobatic display team for the 1963 season.

March 1962
T.5 prototype XM967 (a converted T.4) flies for first time.

Did you know?
The Lightning was phased out of RAF service in June 1988 and disappeared from Kuwaiti and Saudi Arabian service in 1977 and December 1985 respectively, replaced by the Mirage F1 (Kuwait) and the F-15 Eagle (Saudi Arabia).

Did you know?

Few aircraft could outperform the Lightning, and it was not until the F-15 that it had any real competitor. Even the U-2 flying at 85,000ft was not immune from interception as a F.6 could reach almost 88,000ft and on one occasion at least a Lightning pilot not only intercepted the reconnaissance jet but also flew inverted above it – for real, unlike Tom Cruise in Top Gun!

16 June 1962

First prototype F.3 (XP693) flies.

4 November 1962

First F.2 delivered to AFDS at Binbrook.

17 December 1962

19 Squadron at RAF Leconfield becomes first operational RAF squadron to receive the F.2.

Summer 1963

Leconfield Wing becomes fully operational on the F.2.

January 1964

First F.3 production versions enter service with the Central Fighter Establishment (CFE) at Binbrook.

17 April 1964

F.6 prototype (XP697) flies for first time. 74 Squadron at Leuchars becomes first RAF squadron to receive the F.3.

17 July 1964
First production T.5 flies.

18 August 1964
23 Squadron begins replacement with the F.3. At Wattisham, 56 and Treble-One Squadrons begin receiving the F.3 in late 1964.

April 1965
T.5 enters service with 226 OCU at Coltishall.

September-December 1965
19 and 92 Squadrons move to bases eighty miles from the East German border to begin patrolling the air identification zone.

16 November 1965
First F.6 production models issued to AFDS.

10 December 1965
F.6 enters squadron service with 5 Squadron at Binbrook.

Did you know?
By the end of 1977 only 5 and 11 Squadrons remained equipped with the Lightning. The rest of 11 Group's interceptor force had converted from the Lightning to the McDonnell Douglas F-4M Phantom FGR.2. Nos 5 and 11 Squadrons at Binbrook remained equipped with the Lightning until the end of October 1987 and 30 April 1988 respectively.

Did you know?

After 74 Squadron disbanded at Tengah in August 1971, all remaining F.6s fitted with over-wing tanks, or 'overburgers', were flown on the 6,000-mile, thirteen-hour trip to Akrotiri, Cyprus, staging through Gan and Muharraq and completing seven in-flight refuellings with Victor tankers, for transfer to 56 Squadron.

June 1966

Operation *Magic Carpet*.

September 1966

74 'Tiger' Squadron begins conversion to the F.6 from the F.3.

February 1967

Exercise *Forthright 59/60* sees Lightning F.3s flying non-stop to Akrotiri and F.6s returning to the UK, refuelled throughout by Victor tankers.

1 April 1967

11 Squadron re-formed at Leuchars with the F.6. 56 Squadron's Lightnings fly to Cyprus, air-refuelled en route.

1 May 1967

29 Squadron re-forms at Wattisham and becomes the last RAF squadron to equip with the Lightning.

June 1967

Operation *Hydraulic*.

16 January 1968
Total Lightning production reaches 334 (plus five test airframes).

1968
23 Squadron at Leuchars is fully equipped with the F.6.

July 1968
Operation *Magic Palm*.

December 1968
Kuwait Air Force takes delivery of the first F.53s.

1969
RSAF uses Lightnings in offensive action for first time against border positions in Yemen.

Christmas 1969
Exercise *Ultimacy*.

Did you know?
A total of 334 Lightnings were built. Of these 100 were lost in crashes, abandoned, lost in collisions or as a result of enemy action while in service with the RAF, Kuwaiti Air Force (KAF) and Royal Saudi Air Force (RSAF). Nine more were lost on test flights. The worst year for Lightning losses was 1971, when an unlucky thirteen were written off.

5 July 1970
Last F.3A for RAF Germany delivered to 92 Squadron.

Did you know?

It is rumoured that a C-130 of the 36th TAS, USAF, that was taken aloft by a disaffected ground crewman at Mildenhall on 23 May 1969, was shot down in the English Channel near Alderney by a Lightning from Wattisham, sent to intercept the errant Hercules.

25 August 1971
74 Squadron disbanded at Tengah.

September 1974
Treble-One Squadron and 226 OCU both disbanded.

31 December 1974
29 Squadron disbanded.

31 October 1975
23 Squadron disbanded.

31 December 1976
19 Squadron disbanded.

31 March 1977
92 Squadron disbanded.

1977

Kuwait Air Force replaces Lightnings with Mirage F.1Ks

12 January 1986

2 Squadron RSAF is the last Saudi squadron to operate the Lightning.

31 December 1987

5 Squadron disbanded at Binbrook, re-forming as a Tornado F.3 unit on 1 May 1988.

30 April 1988

11 Squadron is the last Lightning squadron to disband, re-forming as a Tornado F.3 Squadron on 1 November 1988.

30 June 1988

Final RAF Lightning flight.

Did you know?

When, in September 1970, a USAF exchange pilot died after his Lightning crashed in the North Sea, Royal Navy divers found the Lightning at a depth of 190ft, almost completely intact with the canopy closed. But the cockpit was empty and the American's body was never found. In the press it was claimed that aliens had abducted him!

Lightning appearing to go through the sound barrier.

◄
*Lightning just before
going into reheat.*

Visit our website and discover thousands of other History Press books.

www.thehistorypress.co.uk